Snakes in Petra

Analecta Gorgiana

1003

Series Editor

George Anton Kiraz

Analecta Gorgiana is a collection of long essays and short monographs which are consistently cited by modern scholars but previously difficult to find because of their original appearance in obscure publications. Carefully selected by a team of scholars based on their relevance to modern scholarship, these essays can now be fully utilized by scholars and proudly owned by libraries.

Snakes in Petra

Robert Wenning

2014

Gorgias Press LLC, 954 River Road, Piscataway, NJ, 08854, USA

www.gorgiaspress.com

G&C Kiraz is an imprint of Gorgias Press LLC

Copyright © 2014 by Gorgias Press LLC

Originally published in 2012

All rights reserved under International and Pan-American Copyright Conventions. No part of this publication may be reproduced, stored in a retrieval system or transmitted in any form or by any means, electronic, mechanical, photocopying, recording, scanning or otherwise without the prior written permission of Gorgias Press LLC.

2014

ISBN 978-1-61719-833-5   ISSN 1935-6854

Extract from *From Ugarit to Nabataea*, edited by G. A. Kiraz and Zeyad Al-Salameen, 235-282 (Gorgias Press, 2012).

Printed and bound by CPI Group (UK) Ltd, Croydon, CR0 4YY

SNAKES IN PETRA

ROBERT WENNING
WESTFÄLISCHE WILHELMS-UNIVERSITÄT MÜNSTER

This article provides some new information about the role of snakes in relation to Nabataean religion, presenting a small group of unknown snake monuments from Petra.

It gives great pleasure to congratulate a dear friend by contributing to his Festschrift. John's book 'The Religion of the Nabataeans' is a stimulating study,[1] and as we share interests in this subject, I would like to present him with a small piece on Nabataean religion.[2] In the book there is no entry for 'snakes' or 'snake-deity', and the present article provides some new information about the role of snakes in Petra.

The aim of this article is not to discuss the complex meaning of snakes in ancient art and religion,[3] but to shed some light on a subject which has received little attention in recent decades, namely the role of snakes in relation to Nabataean religion. This article presents a small group of unknown snake monuments from Petra;[4] first discussing the

---

[1] Healey 2001.

[2] I thank the editors for accepting this paper, and Will Kennedy and Melonie Schmierer for their assistance in providing an English translation.

[3] Glueck 1965: 479–490 and Hammond 1973a: 3–19 (among many others) have discussed in detail various aspects of serpents in Greek and Near Eastern art, emphasizing healing, protection and fecundity in funerary contexts. For pre-Hellenistic snake monuments in the Levant, see Keel 1992: 195–226.

[4] Snakes are also found in Nabataean art from Nabataean settlements apart from Petra, and although these have been considered they are not the subject of the present study.

known snake monuments from Petra (most of which were described and discussed by Dalman in 1908[5]) and how they have been interpreted in the scholarly debate.

THE SNAKE MONUMENT BR. 302 / D. 313

The Snake Monument near the Wādī Rās Sulaymān is the first port of call in any discussion of snakes in Petra. Already mentioned by Irby (1823) and Laborde (1830), with Laborde presenting the first picture of the monument,[6] it is referred to by Brünnow (1904) as a tomb of the Pylon-type with an *omphalus*, decorated with a snake.[7] Dalman (1908) provided the first detailed description of the monument and its setting, followed by a thorough study by Hammond (1973).

Dalman states that the monument is not an altar, tomb or Pylon, but rather a high rock-cut cube crowned with a snake entwined around a cone (Wenning Plate 1: A, B).[8] The cube measures 3.2 x 3.3 x 2.33 m, and the cone is about 2 m high and 2 m in diameter. Glueck has suggested that the cone was a betyl,[9] and Hammond has explained that the coils of the snake did not cover an object in the center.[10] If parallels are considered, one should not exclude the possibility that the snake coils around an imaginary altar.[11] The size of the coils and parallels lead to the conclusion that the snake is a python.

---

[5] Dalman (1908: 76) listed nos. 47d, 210c, 313e, 315. Brünnow and von Domaszweski (1904: 180, 183, 185) mistakenly identified snakes in the reliefs of the Dioscurii, the Nikai and the Amazons of the Khazne, and (179, 319) no.422 in a relief with Eros (see below). This was repeated by Glueck 1965: 483–484.

[6] Ossorio 2009: fig. 66.

[7] Brünnow and von Domaszweski 1904: 144, 162, 287, 289 no. 302, fig. 143, with citations of Irby and Laborde; Jeremias 1907: 167. The drawing fig. 143 is criticized by Dalman 1908: 217 note 3.

[8] Dalman 1908: 76, 217–219 no. 313, figs. 141–144. The cone was already mentioned by Irby.

[9] Glueck 1965: 483. He calls it a 'Dushara block'. This is repeated by Hammond 1973: 2–3, 25–29.

[10] Hammond 1973a: 2.

[11] Comparison with examples from Rhodes in Weber 1996: 14; 1997: 117 assumes a cylindrical altar or upper part.

The head was mistakenly assumed to be part of the thick upper part, which is actually part of the upper coil.[12] In fact, the head of the snake was most likely on the top, which seems to be lost. The second and third coils below the upper part have been destroyed at the western side, and this was already visible in the figures of Dalman over 100 years ago.[13] Today, the upper coil appears to overlap the damaged part giving a misleading impression of a large mouth. As the head has in fact been lost, one should not follow Dalman's assumption that the head of the snake is oriented towards the southwest;[14] and Hammond's suggestion that the snake was placed in the direction of the necropolis[15] may very well be the case.

Dalman mentions cuttings on the cube and a platform belonging to the monument (Wenning Plate 1: D), and Hammond notes that parts of the monument have never been finished.[16] He describes the approach to the monument as a 'processional way', but although a path to the monument exists, to describe it as a 'processional way' seems somewhat unconvincing and over-interpreted. Hammond himself remarks that the very limited size of the monument's platform could not accommodate many people at the same time, and that there is no indication of a cultic apparatus.[17]

The Snake Monument is part of the necropolis between the head of Wādī Thugra and Rās Sulaymān about 1.25 km south of Petra, and is cut into the rock of a very high peak overlooking the area of the necropolis (Wenning Plate 1: C). Behind the monument, part of the peak is still untouched at the same height as the monument. Although the peak of the promontory is in the very southeast of the rocky area, it is in a prominent position. Hammond refers to it as a commanding height.[18] Taking into account the Block Tombs Br. 303 and 307, and the shape, style and workmanship of the monument (block-like composi-

---

12 Dalman 1908: 218.
13 Dalman 1908: fig. 142.
14 Dalman 1908: 218.
15 Hammond 1973a: 3, 20. Dalman 1908: 217–218 notes that the cube is oriented in accordance with cardinal points.
16 Hammond 1973a: 22–23.
17 Hammond 1973a: 2, 19–20.
18 Hammond 1973a: 19.

tion, crude modeling, complete lack of elaboration and some unfinished details), Hammond associates the necropolis and Snake Monument with the earliest funerary monuments at Petra (2nd c. BCE to 1st c. BCE).[19] Although Hammond's dating seems correct, the block-like composition is already found in prototypes.[20] One must also consider the poor state of preservation of the monument and the possibility that the snake could have been plastered and painted. Unfinished parts of monuments, especially those near to the ground, are not a criterion for dating.[21]

Dalman interprets the snake as a chthonic animal, functioning as a guardian of the cave tomb (which he assumed to be below the monument).[22] Zayadine (1975) also mentions a cave.[23] Hammond rejects the possibility of a tomb being related to the monument, assuming that the massive Snake Monument was a 'public' monument to protect the whole necropolis.[24] He compares the role of the snake as a protector

---

19 Hammond 1973a: 22–27. Hammond 1992, 262 also tried to place the earliest phase of the settlement in Petra in this southern area. His thesis of a settlement here is not convincing, but the necropolis could depend on the new settlement of the Nabataean nobility in Petra itself in this period. The same situation can be observed in the Bāb as-Sīq in the east of Petra. The early dating can be supported by the results of Isabelle Sachet's excavation of Block Tomb Br. 303 in 2006. She is preparing a publication and kindly sent me an unpublished report on this research. She dates the earliest phase of this tomb to the late 2nd c. BCE (Sachet 2010: 159).

20 See Weber 1997: figs. 129b-c.

21 For example, the Khazne shows a range of unfinished parts and details.

22 The interpretation of Robinson 1930: 81–82 with some biblical connotations was a setback. He reported that the monument represented a kind of serpent worship, older than all other altars, shrines and sanctuaries in Petra, potentially even Edomite in origin. This classification is not acceptable.

23 Zayadine 1975: 336. It remains unclear exactly which cave is meant by Dalman and Zayadine. Jeremias 1907: 167 refers to the pedestal. The cave at the foot of the rock drawn by Laborde (Ossorio 2009: fig. 66) appears to be a fiction. There are some hollows in the rock, but none of these seems to be a burial cave. Therefore, it could be that Dalman and Zayadine refer to Block Tomb Br. 303 (D. 310), which is situated about 25 m southeast of the Snake Monument. Isabelle Sachet kindly provided me with a plan of the area, and there is no other tomb or burial cave included except Br. 303.

24 Hammond 1973a: 19–21, 23; Sachet presented a paper at the XI International Conference on the Archaeology and History of Jordan at Paris, June 2010,

with Tyche, the protective goddess governing the fortune and prosperity of cities.[25]

Although the monument is sculpted figuratively, Hammond interprets the monument as a kind of 'sacred stone'. He compares the cube not only with the Block Tombs but also with betyls.[26] This focus on the cube rather than the snake is problematic, as the cube is just the pedestal of the snake.[27]

With Glueck's interpretation of the Khirbat at-Tannur sculptures in mind, Hammond discusses Nabataean betyls in combination with eagles and eagles with serpents. Accepting the notion that the eagle is a symbol of the sun god Dushara, he concludes that in the earliest stages the sun god was represented by the snake motif alone, and that the snake might be a surrogate of Dushara as sun god or even the oldest representation of Dushara.[28] Assuming that the snake was a divine symbol, Hammond envisions a cultic setting for the monument.[29] However, there are too many uncertainties in his thesis and it cannot be accepted.[30]

Another avenue for interpretation is suggested by Zayadine, who notes the existence of a parallel monument from Gadara.[31] The Gadara snake monument, which belongs to a rock-cut tomb, was classified by

---

suggesting that the snake could also have been the protector of the southern entrance to Petra, which seems less convincing to me.

25 Hammond (1973a: 11) refers to the personal name Naḥaštab as the 'good serpent', an epithet of the Minaean god Wadd, following Savignac 1933: 413; Höfner 1965b: 518. Others explain the name as 'the good fortune', without relating it to a snake-god. The name is documented in Nabataean inscriptions at Wādī Ramm, Ruwāfah, Ḥegra, and Petra (Negev 1991: no. 723; Milik and Starcky 1975: 127).

26 Hammond 1973a: 23–29. For an overview of Nabataean betyls compare Wenning 2001.

27 Because the monument follows Greek prototypes, the cube as the carrier of the figure can hardly be compared with the mōtab, which is the carrier or 'seat' of the betyls (Healey 2001: 158–159; Wenning 2001: 88–90).

28 Hammond 1973a: 25–29; 1973b: 50–51.

29 Hammond 1973a: 21.

30 See as well Zayadine 1980: 219; Zayadine 1983: 187, pl. 9A.

31 Zayadine 1983: 187, pl. 9C.

Weber, and dated to the 2nd c. BCE.[32] Weber cites a large group of snake monuments, giving special emphasis to those with a funerary context. He refers to Hellenistic funerary monuments from Rhodes and Rheneia, and as Nabataeans are documented at Rhodes in the Hellenistic period,[33] these Hellenistic monuments could very well have been the prototype for the Petra and Gadara monuments.

As Weber explains, the snake was the apotropaic symbol of foreign metics (resident aliens) at Rhodes and the south-western littoral zone of Asia Minor in the Late Hellenistic period. Metics did not have full civil rights, and were organized in separate associations which took care of the burials and sepulchral representations of their members. This does not, however, mean that the monument in Petra was attached to foreign individual, as the type of monument could have been adopted by a Nabataean.

One should not then assume that the monument involved veneration of the snake, that the Snake Monument was a 'public monument', or that it represented the protector of the whole necropolis in this area. It does not represent 'good fortune', the *agathos daimon*, the 'good genius', and of course does not represent Dushara. The main aspect of the snake should be seen as apotropaic. This interpretation is supported by snake representations on Nabataean tombs in Ḥegra.[34]

Any interpretation of the Snake Monument should include the Block tomb Br. 303. Both are monumental, both seem to have an early date, and they are the only installations in that corner of the necropolis. If this suggestion is correct, the Snake Monument should be seen as a monumental tomb marker, not in the sense of the *nefesh*,[35] but in the

---

[32] Weber 2002: 413–414 no. PL 28, pl. 46 E; 1996: 13–14, pl. 5 A-B; 1997: 117–118, figs.129a-c.

[33] Wenning 1987: 23 no. A 8; Roche 1996: 78, 85; D. Graf read a paper on the Nabataeans in the Mediterranean at the XI International Conference on the Archaeology and History of Jordan at Paris, June 2010.

[34] The tombs B 1, 7, 11, 22, and 23 show an apotropaic mask or face (Humbaba) between two snakes in the pediment (McKenzie 1990: pl. 2–4, 16; McKenzie, Reyes and Schmidt-Colinet 1998: 39–41, figs. 7, 9). The tombs are dated to the second quarter of the 1st c. CE.

[35] See Kühn 2005 for the meaning of *nefesh* in ancient Near Eastern cultures and for a catalogue of *nefesh* monuments in Petra.

sense of an individual representative monument (as in the prototypes at Rhodes).

THE RELIEF D. 47E

A clear sepulchral context is given for a relief in the small, low tomb D. 47 in the Bāb as-Sīq. The floor of the cave is densely filled with graves. The entrance wall in the interior has two reliefs discovered by Dalman.[36] To the left is a horse or mule carrying a betyl (D. 47d),[37] and to the right are two snakes with a quadruped between their heads (D. 47e).[38]

The snakes wind diagonally to the upper right corner with their tails touching each other (Wenning Plate 2: A), giving the impression of a kind of enclosure or gable hurdle for the animal at the top. The bodies of the snakes coil slightly and become larger towards the top. The snakes measure 1.53 m and 1.62 m. From their size and thickness (5–15 cm), and size relative to the quadruped, the snakes appear to be pythons. The head of the left snake is at the height of the bowed head of the quadruped, preventing the animal from escaping. The right snake is biting into a hind leg of the quadruped and trying to pull the animal backwards to devour it. The quadruped measures 35 x 17 cm. The tail of the animal is raised. It is impossible to give a precise classification of the quadruped; a dog or a bull was suggested by Dalman, a jackal by Zayadine.[39] Dalman assumes the scene has a protective function and Zayadine assumes it to be apotropaic. Both associations seem possible and are not mutually exclusive. If the scene represents a mythological tale, it is unknown.[40]

THE RELIEF D. 210E

Dalman grouped together the monuments D. 207–D. 219 in his 'second sanctuary of the theater mountain'. This grouping and interpretation is debatable, although a sanctuary could fit in the rock-cut

---

[36] Dalman 1908: 76, 110 no. 47e, fig. 28.
[37] Wenning 2001: 91, fig. 8.
[38] Nehmé and Villeneuve 1999: fig. 25.
[39] Zayadine 1974: 43.
[40] Kühn 2005: 69, 277. Contrary to Glueck 1965: 484 the snake and dog in this relief do not refer to Mithraic symbols.

chamber D. 210. The monuments are situated on the upper terrace of the so-called northern way to the Great High Place. Today it is almost impossible to continue from this terrace to the summit, and this may explain why D. 210 received almost no attention after its first description by Dalman in 1908.[41]

The back wall of chamber D. 210 has a very large niche (2.05 x 2.26 m) reaching to the ceiling (Wenning Plate 2: B). A profiled pedestal 1.42 cm long and 53 cm high (D. 210d) joins the niche to the right and continues all the way to the lateral side. A snake (D. 210e) is cut in high relief above the pedestal (Wenning Plate 2: C). In the wall above the snake are two empty votive niches (D. 210f). It was usual to set up betyls in niches on certain occasions. It can be assumed that there was a relationship between the snake on the pedestal and the niches, unless one prefers to relate the niches to whatever was installed in the central niche. The contents of the central niche remain unknown.[42] There are no niches or reliefs at the left of the central niche.

The lower profile of the pedestal is directly below the bottom line of the great niche, although the reason for that arrangement remains unknown. The upper profile is badly damaged. Large parts are cut away irregularly, and it appears as if someone had once tried to carve another snake. A draped female figure is sculptured at the body of the pedestal at a distance of 31.5 cm from the left edge (Wenning Plate 2: D). The tall figure measures 32 cm in height. She is moving to the left and is shown in three-quarter view. The folds of the *chiton* and *himation* are clearly visible. The head of the figure once touched the upper profile, but is now cut off. The figure is so badly preserved that it is very difficult to classify her.[43]

---

[41] Dalman 1908: 185–187, figs. 101–103; Lindner 1976, 93, fig. on p. 93.

[42] Dalman 1908: 186 cautiously suggested two statues, but the two holes in the back wall of the niche do not support such a conclusion. A niche with two statues would be decidedly unexpected in Petra, and there are very few examples of high niches with a statue like that suggested in the so-called Obodas chapel (D. 294b).

[43] Helmut Merklein suggested Isis in a personal communication in 1995. The figure is not winged or horned, is not fish-tailed, and does not appear to have an outstretched arm. The poor state of preservation and insufficient documentation advises against such interpretations.

The snake is not resting directly upon the pedestal, but is winding horizontally slightly above it. A festoon is painted between the upper profile of the pedestal and the coils of the snake. The snake winds from right to left and is oriented to the main niche. The end of the snake's tail is sculptured horizontally on the lateral wall. The complete length of the snake is 1.85 m, and the body measures up to a maximum of 13 cm in height. After four coils the body of the snake is raised diagonally, but the head has been cut away.[44] Once again, the snake can probably be identified as a python.

Dalman assumes the snake to be an object of divine veneration.[45] It seems the most convincing interpretation because of the pedestal, the figure on the pedestal and the festoon, but the snake could also have been a protective power; a guardian related to deities in the central niche. Lindner recalls the *lararium* of the House of the Vettii in Pompeii, terms the snake 'the good spirit of the house', and assumes figurines of *Lares* in the niches.[46] In my opinion there are too many differences between the two monuments, which do not support the comparison or its associations.

SNAKES AS ATTRIBUTES

Hermes/Mercury

Hermes/Mercury holding the *kerykeion* or *caduceus* (a rod with two winding snakes), is depicted in three bust reliefs and a medallion relief from Petra.[47] In mythology the snakes fought each other until Hermes separated them, and in gratitude they entwined his rod, and became a symbol of freedom and trade. The Nabataeans, however, seem to have preferred a *kerykeion* with snakes fighting aggressively.

---

44 The impression that the body thickens towards the head and that the mouth was wide open is only due to damage.

45 Dalman 1908: 76.

46 Lindner 1976: 93, with a sketch of the lararium on page 94. By the same measure one could compare the snake below Mithras as Tauroktonos (like Merkelbach 1984: fig. 50), but both belong to a different tradition.

47 Wenning 2004: nos. 9.1, 10.3, 12.3; B.1.3.

Athena

Athena wears the powerful *aegis*, the skin of a goat with snake oracles and the head of Medusa in the center. Athena, or Athena Allat, is depicted with the *aegis* in four bust reliefs from Petra.[48]

Medusa

In mythology the head of Medusa, the *Gorgoneion*, turned to stone all who gazed upon her. The hero Perseus beheaded Medusa, and her snake-haired head became a prominent apotropaic sign in Greek art from the 8th c. BCE onward. The fearful face is emphasized rather than the snakes, which shape a knot around the neck. There are at least 28 representations of the *Gorgoneion* known from Petra, mostly with a more decorative function.[49] As Grawehr discusses, these *Gorgoneia* probably do not contain any local features, and they are unrelated to other snake monuments from Petra.[50] None of these three groups with snakes as attributes are associated with the role of snakes in Petra.

FRIEZE, EROTES WITH SNAKE-LIKE *TAENIA* (BR. 422, D. 863–864)

Brünnow and von Domaszewski and Dalman discovered two reliefs of Erotes between winged lions and griffins[51], and a fragment of a third relief was exhibited in the yard of the Archaeological Museum in Petra in 1995.[52] Bachmann, Watzinger and Wiegand attribute the reliefs to

---

[48] Wenning 2004: nos. 12.4, 13.9; Stucky 1996: 340 nos. 32–33.

[49] In architecture: the Khazne (McKenzie 1990: pl. 83a), the Lion Triclinium (McKenzie 1990: pl. 136b), Tomb Br. 649 (Freyberger 1998: pl. 71d), and the Tomb of Sextius Florentinus (McKenzie, Reyes and Schmidt-Colinet 1998: 39, fig. 5c), the Temple of the Winged Lions-complex (Wagner 2001: fig. 2); in figural capitals (Parr 1957: pls. 8B, 13B; Kolb and Keller1999: frontispiece; Bikai et al. 2008: figs. 15h-i); in the *oscilla* of the fresco from az-Zanṭur (Kolb 2003: fig. 260); in weapon-friezes (McKenzie 1990: pls. 64b, 65b; McKenzie, Reyes and Schmidt-Colinet 1998: fig. 5a); fragment of relief or a statue of Athena-Allat (Donner and Sieg 1998: fig.28); on lamps (Rosenthal and Siwan 1978: fig. no. 396; Grawehr 2010: pl. 6).

[50] Grawehr 2010: 223–225.

[51] Brünnow and von Domaszewski 1904: 178–179, 319 no. 422, fig. 348; Jeremias 1907: 175; Dalman 1908: 76, 354–356 nos. 863–864, figs. 324–325.

[52] McKenzie 1988: 93 no. 42.

the entrance of the *Ephebeion* in the north of the lower yard of the assumed *Gymnasium*.[53] It subsequently became clear that this forms part of the access way to the Temple of the Winged Lions. The first explorers described the Erotes as having snakes in their hands and compared that motif with the infant Heracles strangling snakes and the apotropaic stelae of Horus holding snakes and other dangerous animals in his hands.

Bachmann, Watzinger and Wiegand, however, correctly recognized the supposed 'snakes' to be *taenia*, strips of fabric. Although *taenia* could be used to honor victors, they are used here by the Erotes to bind mythical animals. The composition was still an adaption of the old motif of the *potnos theron*, now embedded into Hellenistic style and thinking. Although the strips are perhaps intentionally shaped in a snake-like fashion, the reliefs in Petra do not represent snakes and do not refer to snakes in Petra.[54]

PETROGLYPHS

There may be some depictions of snakes among the petroglyphs in Petra, but these monuments have not yet been fully documented. Dalman noticed an incision (D. 315) near the Snake Monument,[55] but it is debatable whether a snake is actually represented. Lindner mentions an incised snake near the Isis sanctuary at the Wādī Abū ʾOllēqa.[56] U. Hübner kindly sent me a photograph of a snake carved into a piece of rock, which he discovered at the western base of Umm al-Biyāra (Wenning Plate 3: A).[57] The stone is somewhat eroded and measures about 48 x 30 x 10 cm. The snake, a viper, is directed to the right and is uprising while coiling heavily. These petroglyphs can only be dated roughly (and may be Nabataean, Roman, or even Byzantine). It cannot be assumed that they are Nabataean in the strictest sense.

---

[53] Bachmann, Watzinger and Wiegand 1921:65–67, fig. 59.

[54] A snake-like handle is attached to a Nabataean cup (Horsfield 1941: 138–139 no. 135, pl. 19). It seems to be more of an artistic variant of the twisted handles than a meaningful representation of snakes.

[55] Dalman 1908: 219 no. 315, fig. 144.

[56] Lindner 1989: 288.

[57] Ulrich Hübner, personal communication in 2010. I am grateful for this information and the permission to include the find in this article.

THE NEW GROUP OF SNAKE MONUMENTS

Rock-cut relief in al-Qanṭara

In 2007 D. Kühn kindly reported seeing a snake relief in the Wādī al-Qanṭara to me, and I was able to visit the spot later that year.[58] The relief seems to be known to the Bedouins and some guides, but is not yet mentioned in scholarly studies. To reach the site, one starts at Dalman's so-called 'second sanctuary of al-Qanṭara' (D. 123) and climbs down into the Wādī al-Qanṭara, which is divided here into two river beds. One continues about 150 m to the east to reach the most southern bank of the Wādī al-Qanṭara. To the left there is the rock-face with the snake relief (coordinates: x735.826, y356.586, UTM). The shallow relief is cut about 60 cm above a rocky ledge and measures 39 cm in width and 64 cm in height (Wenning Plate 3: B). The outline of the niche is a very shallow and slightly eroded depression.

The steeply uprising snake is depicted in three slight coils (Wenning Plate 3: C). The tail is not resting on the ground. The body is somewhat flat with clear edges and the snake is oriented to the left. It is not easy to define where the mouth ends, and the head does not seem to widen greatly. In front of the head of the snake there is something which cannot be identified.[59] It is also difficult to classify the type of the snake. It is not a cobra (*uraeus*), and probably not a python. It could be a viper. The snake does not threaten, but rather seems to have a protective character. It does not belong to the types of the snakes representing the *genius loci* or the *agathos daimon*. The best parallel is that of the harmless snake of Aesculapius. Although one must assume that the Nabataeans used a prototype for the relief, it is not possible to deter-

---

[58] Dagmar Kühn provided me with a photograph, and this find prompted me to give attention to the snake monuments in Petra. I am very grateful for her information.

[59] The object hangs like a garland. It is not clear if the snake is attacking or devouring an animal. It is also possible that the snake is touching an object. The mouth and uprising coiling of the snake give a wrong impression of being a seahorse instead of a snake. The outlines of the niche and the snake are damaged by modern scratches. An incised number 6 to the right and a circle to the left of the relief are either accidental or secondary.

mine where the prototype came from. It is my impression that it seems more Hellenistic than Egyptian or Near Eastern.

The monument's size and the way the niche is cut and positioned correspond with Nabataean votive niches, among which these snake reliefs are rather unusual. Although there are no other installations around this niche and nearby, which is not uncommon among the votive niches in Petra, the setting could support an assumption of veneration. Snakes' annual shedding of their skin rendered them a symbol of regeneration and everlasting life. Much about this snake monument remains uncertain. It is unknown whether the snake was intended to protect from snake-bites like the biblical Nehushtan (Num 21:8–9), which, like Aesculapius' snake, was associated with healing.[60] If this snake monument is indeed related to a particular deity, we must agree with Dalman that much remains uncertain.[61]

Rock-cut relief near the stairs to Umm al-Biyāra

In 2010 I showed S. G. Schmid a photograph of the snake relief discussed above and asked him if he knew of any other snake monuments in Petra. Fortuitously, he recalled seeing a small relief of a snake while climbing up to Umm al-Biyāra a few days before. He kindly provided me with a photograph taken during the discovery (Wenning Plate 3: D).[62] In 2011 I was able to relocate the relief, which is unusually near to the restored stairs, just 25 cm above them, and almost at the bottom of the cliff. It is a very small relief, 7 cm in width and 18 cm in height. The relief of the snake and the rectangular niche-like hollow are so flat that it was not possible to measure the depth. The relief is slightly eroded and has become indistinct.

The relief is that of the al-Qanṭara relief *en miniature*. The snake is steeply uprising in three slight coils and the tail barely touches the ground. The snake is oriented to the left. The body of the snake is

---

[60] In the Syrian sphere *Šadrapaʾ* should be added (Lichtenberger 2003: 44–46, 312).

[61] Dalman 1908: 76; Höfner 1965a: 442. There are various deities connected with snakes, like Wadd or Nergal, but it is not yet possible to identify the Nabataean deity venerated here.

[62] I am grateful to Stephan G. Schmid for the information, the photograph and the kind permission to include his find in this article.

somewhat flat and the head is slightly enlarged and may possibly be used to clarify the head of the al-Qanṭara snake.

To the left of the snake there seems to be an incised horned altar, which is even closer to the stairs. The altar is as worn and indistinct as the snake relief and is scratched rather than neatly incised. The upper right part has flaked off.

To the left of the two carvings is a worn Nabataean šlm-inscription with a personal name.[63] Directly above the snake relief and below a protruding part of the rock is a votive niche (Wenning Plate 4: A). It measures 32 x 42–47 x 16.5 cm. The back wall is slightly curved and parts have flaked off. The ceiling and the lateral sides of the niche are also damaged. In front of the bottom is a small cup-like hollow (8 x 8 x 6 cm) for libations. The niche is empty. Directly to the left is a second niche (32 x ca. 26 x 7 cm), which is more worn. This niche is also empty.

It can be assumed that the two niches are related to the snake relief, but this remains uncertain considering the different sizes. People walking up will readily notice the niches, but may easily overlook the snake relief. There is no obvious answer accounting for the size of the snake relief and its location.

Rock-cut relief at Jabal al-Barra

In 2010 I heard of a snake relief in Jabal al-Barra, an area believed to be lacking Nabataean niches and inscriptions. I had the opportunity to conduct a day-long survey of the area and discovered several Nabataean monuments, among them the snake relief. This area seems to be well-known to Bedouins and hikers, and the place has been used as a spot for coffee-breaks and has suffered thoughtless damage.[64]

The snake relief, a niche and two Nabataean inscriptions are cut into the rock-face below a protruding part of the rock (coordinates: x0733.283, y3357.443). In front of the niches is a plateau opposite the

---

[63] Laïla Nehmé kindly read it šlm tymw (personal communication, 2011), and noticed another šlm-inscription to the right of the first one. I am grateful for her help.

[64] There are scratches to the snake relief and damage on the inscription and the niche. On both sides of the snake relief there are several modern Arab names scratched on the rock.

southwest end of Umm al-Biyāra. There are no other installations except for a small basin (34 x 22 x 6–12 cm) in the rock-floor about 30 m to the east, where a small buried gorge with a large crevice comes down from the south. The plateau is situated to the western end of the massif. There is another valley beyond it and from the next height one can see down to the 'Araba. Before one climbs into the valley, Rās Slaysil is visible in the northeast.

The flat snake relief measures 41–50 cm in width and 147 cm in height (Wenning Plate 4: B). The edges of the original niche can be seen in the two upper corners, directly joined by the inscriptions. The lower left edge cannot be determined with certainty, as the framing is arched and is not symmetrical to the upper part. It is possible that the niche was unfinished or was poorly worked at this point. The snake is steeply uprising in six coils. The long tail rests on the ground to the right, while the snake is directed to the left. The body is relatively broad. The coiling is somewhat irregular in comparison with the other two reliefs. The outline of the snake has been retraced by modern scratches. Although the head is not enlarged, the snake appears to resemble a cobra more than a viper, although in comparison with the other reliefs one should assume that all three snakes belong to the same kind (possibly a viper). This snake is not defined by the type of other contexts.[65] However, it is possible that no such classification was intended, and that it was sufficient to depict a snake, a mighty image of power.

A smaller niche is cut into the niche of the snake just in front and to the left of the head of the snake (Wenning Plate 4: C). The niche measures 22 cm in width, 29 cm in height, and 17 cm in depth at the bottom of the niche. The back of the niche is arched like an abutment niche. The back and the lateral sides are roughly chiseled. It is possible that only the floor of the niche is original and that the niche was enlarged and deepened in later or modern times. Directly below the niche joining the right lower edge is a hollow (11 x 10 x 6 cm), which seems to have originally been cut for libations.

---

[65] It is possible to find a few parallels for these uprising snakes, but a connection cannot be established. The back of an altar from the Mithraeum of S. Clemente in Rome depicts such a snake, representing the second grade (Merkelbach 1984: 91, fig. 45).

The Nabataean inscription to the right of the snake relief measures 24 x 24 cm and is carved slightly slanting (Wenning Plate 4: D). It was read as *ḥplw?* by L. Nehmé. The Nabataean inscription to the left of the snake relief measures 33 x 7 cm (Wenning Plate 4: C), and is disturbed by two secondary holes drilled into two characters. It was read as *ʾly. šhw{ʾ}?* by L. Nehmé.[66] Both inscriptions do not explain the relief or the meaning of the snake, but could well have been carved by worshippers.

In summary, the Nabataeans were very familiar with use of snake imagery in monuments and reliefs. All monuments refer to individual religious practices of the Nabataeans and range in size from small to monumental. Although the function of the snake monuments was apotropaic-protective, especially within sepulchral contexts where no veneration of the snakes seems intended, the snakes were clearly an object of cultic veneration, probably concerned with protection. These monuments can be grouped together with votive niches with betyls and figural deities (e.g. Isis, Dushara-bust, and eagle), and it is significant that from among these a specific type developed around the snake. Two of the monuments seem to depict a scene from a narrative (D. 47e, D. 210e). As no Nabataean mythological texts are known, we are unlikely to be able to explain these contexts or even to tell which deity the snakes represent. However, this new group of monuments does support the idea of a snake cult or snake-deity in Petra.

BIBLIOGRAPHY

Bachmann, W., C. Watzinger and T. Wiegand
1921, *Petra* (Berlin).

Brünnow, R.-E. and A. von Domaszewski
1904, *Die Provincia Arabia auf Grund zweier in den Jahren 1897 und 1898 unternommenen Reisen und der Berichte früherer Reisender beschrieben*, vol. I (Strassburg).

Dalman, G.
1908, *Petra und seine Felsheiligtümer* (Leipzig).

---

[66] Laïla Nehmé kindly gave me her first readings based on my photographs (personal communication).

Donner, H. and E. Sieg
1998, 'Observations and Investigations in the Upper Valley of the Hermitage near ad- Dayr, Petra', *Annual of the Department of Antiquities of Jordan* 42, pp. 279–292.

Freyberger, K. S.
1998, *Die frühkaiserzeitlichen Heiligtümer der Karawanenstationen im hellenisierten Osten. Damaszener Forschungen* 6 (Mainz).

Glueck, N.
1965, *The story of the Nabataeans. Deities and Dolphins* (New York).

Grawehr, M.
2010, *Eine Bronzewerkstatt des 1. Jhs. n. Chr. von ez Zantur in Petra/Jordanien*, Petra Ez Zantur, vol. IV (Mainz).

Hammond, P. C.
1973a, 'The Snake Monument at Petra', *American Journal of Arabic Studies* 1, pp. 1–29.
1973b, *The Nabataeans: Their History, Culture and Archaeology* (Gothenburg).
1992, 'Nabataean Settlement Patterns inside Petra', *Studies in the History and Archaeology of Jordan* 4, pp. 261–262.

Healey, J. F.
2001, *The Religion of the Nabataeans. A Conspectus* (Leiden).

Höfner, M.
1965a, 'Die Stammesgruppen Nord- und Zentralarabiens in vorislamischer Zeit', in H. W. Haussig (ed), *Götter und Mythen im Vorderen Orient* (Stuttgart), pp. 407–481.
1965b, 'Südarabien (Sabaʾ, Qatabān u.a.)', in H. W. Haussig (ed), *Götter und Mythen im Vorderen Orient* (Stuttgart), pp. 483–552.

Horsfield, G. and A. Conway
1941, 'Sela-Petra, The Rock, of Edom and Nabatene IV. The Finds', *Quarterly of the Department of Antiquities of Palestine* 9, pp. 105–204.

Jeremias, F.
1907, *Nach Petra!* Palästinajahrbuch des Deutschen Evangelischen Instituts für Altertumswissenschaft des Heiligen Landes zu Jerusalem 3, pp. 151–174.

Keel, O.
1992, *Das Recht der Bilder gesehen zu warden* (Freiburg/Schweiz).

Kolb B.
2003, 'Petra – From Tent to Mansion: Living on the Terraces of Ez-Zantur', in G. Markoe (ed), *Petra Rediscovered. Lost City of the Nabataeans* (New York), pp. 230–237.

Kolb, B. and D. Keller
1999, 'Schweizerisch-Liechtensteinische Ausgrabungen auf ez Zantur in Petra 1999', *Jahresbericht der Schweizerisch-Liechtensteinische Stiftung für archäologische Forschungen im Ausland 1999*, pp. 17–34.

Kühn, D.
2005, *Totengedenken bei den Nabatäern und im Alten Testament* (Münster).

Lichtenberger, A.
2003, *Kulte und Kultur der Dekapolis. Untersuchungen zu numismatischen, archäologischen und epigraphischen Zeugnissen* (Wiesbaden).

Lindner, M.
1976, 'Die zweite archäologische Expedition der Naturhistorischen Gesellschaft nach Petra (1976)', *Natur und Mensch. Jahresmitteilungen der Naturhistorischen Gesellschaft Nürnberg e.V*, pp. 83–96.
1989, 'Ein nabatäisches Klammheiligtum bei Petra', in M. Lindner (ed), *Petra und das Königreich der Nabatäer* (5th ed.) (Nürnberg), pp. 286–292.

McKenzie, J. S.
1988, 'The Development of Nabataean Sculpture at Petra and Khirbet Tannur', *Palestine Exploration Quarterly* 120, pp. 81–107.
1990, *The Architecture of Petra* (Oxford).

McKenzie, J. S., A. T. Reyes and A. Schmidt-Colinet
1998, 'Faces in the Rock at Petra and Medain Saleh', *Palestine Exploration Quarterly* 130, pp. 35–50.

Merkelbach, R.
1984, *Mithras* (Königstein).

Milik, J. T. and J. Starcky
1975, 'Inscriptions récemment découvertes à Pétra', *Annual of the Department of Antiquities of Jordan* 20, pp. 111–130.

Negev, A.
1991, *Personal Names in the Nabtean Realm* (Jerusalem).

Nehmé, L. and F. Villeneuve
1999, *Pétra: Métropole de l'arabie antique* (Paris).

Ossorio, F. A.
2009, *Petra. Splendors of the Nabataean Civilization* (Vercelli).

Robinson, G. L.
1930, *The Sarcophagus of an Ancient Civilization: Petra, Edom, and the Edomites* (New York).

Roche, M.-J.
1996, 'Remarques sur les Nabatéens en Méditerranée', *Semitica* 45, pp. 73–99.

Rosenthal, R. and R. Sivan
1978, *Ancient Lamps in the Schloessinger Collection* (Jerusalem).

Sachet, I.
2010, 'Libations funéraires aux frontières de l'Orient romain: le cas de la Nabatène', in J. Rüpke and J. Scheid (eds), *Bestattungsrituale und Totenkult in der römischen Kaiserzeit* (Stuttgart), pp. 157–174.

Savignac, R.
1933, 'Le sanctuaire d'Allat à Iram', *Revue Biblique* 42, pp. 405–422.

Stucky, R. A.
1996, 'Ausgewählte Kleinfunde', in A. Bignasca *et al* (eds), *Petra. Ez Zantur I. Ergebnisse der Schweizerisch-Liechtensteinischen Ausgrabungen 1988–1992* (Mainz), pp. 337–353.

Wagner, M.
2001, 'Ein neues Fundstück aus dem großen Petra-Puzzle. Natur und Mensch', *Jahresmitteilungen der Naturhistorischen Gesellschaft* (Nürnberg) e.V, pp. 309–322.

Weber, T.
1996, 'Gadarenes in Exile', *Zeitschrift des Deutschen Palästina-Vereins* 112, pp. 10–17.

1997, 'Die Bildkunst der Nabatäer', in T. Weber and R. Wenning (eds), *Petra. Antike Felsstadt zwischen arabischer Tradition und griechischer Norm* (Mainz), pp. 114–125.
2002, *Gadara – Umm Qēs Vol. I. Gadara Decapolitana. Untersuchungen zur Topographie, Geschichte, Architektur und bildenden Kunst einer "Polis Hellenis" im Ostjordanland. Abhandlungen des Deutschen Palästina-Vereins 30* (Wiesbaden).

Wenning, R.
1987, *Die Nabatäer. Denkmäler und Geschichte* (Freiburg/Schweiz).
2001, 'The Betyls of Petra', *Bulletin of the American Schools of Oriental Research* 324, pp. 79–95.
2004, 'Nabatäische Büstenreliefs aus Petra. Zwei Neufunde, mit U. Hübner', *Zeitschrift des Deutschen Palästina-Vereins* 120, pp. 157–181.

Zayadine, F.
1974, 'Die Felsarchitektur Petras', in M. Lindner (ed), *Petra und das Königreich der Nabatäer* (2nd ed.) (Nürnberg), pp. 39–69.
1975, 'Un ouvrage sur les Nabatéens', *Revue Archéologique* 70, pp. 333–338.
1980, 'Die Felsarchitektur Petras', in M. Lindner (ed), *Petra und das Königreich der Nabatäer* (3rd ed.) (Nürnberg), pp. 212–248.
1983, 'Un fascinum près de l'Odéon d'Amman-Philadelphie', *Zeitschrift des Deutschen Palästina-Vereins* 99, pp. 184–188.

Figures

Al Fassi Plate 1: Tomb of Kamkam, the Priestess B19: JS 16; H 16 (photo J. Healey)

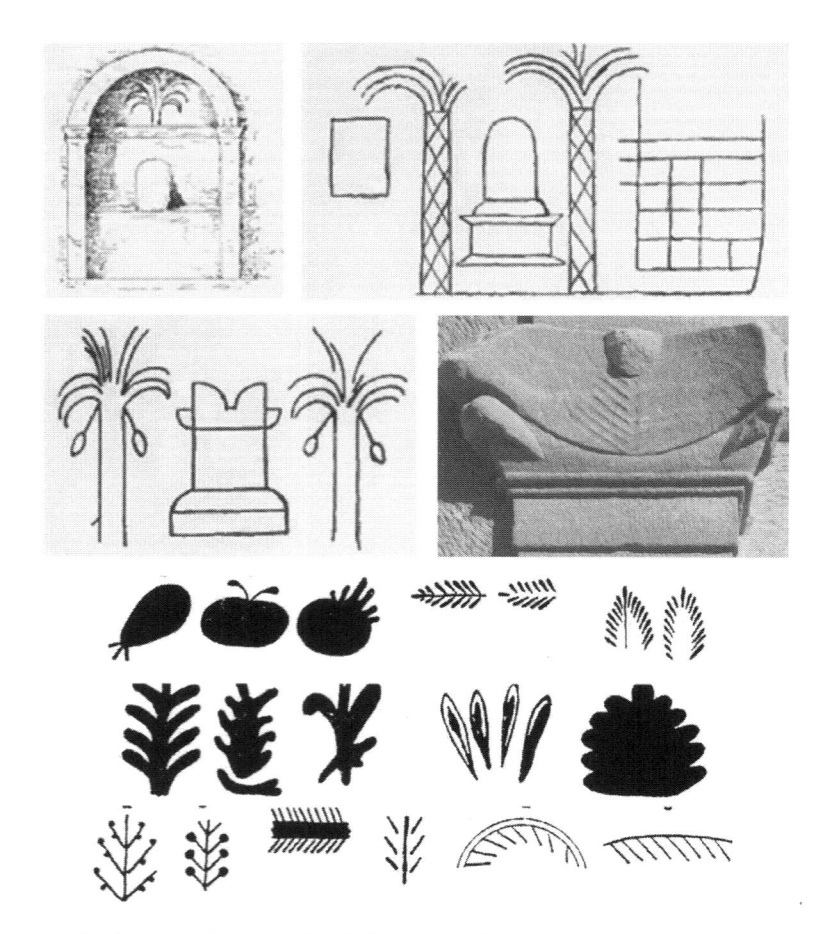

Al-Salameen Plate 1: A (*top left*): Idol-niche in the Siq, Petra (Dalman 1912: 45); B (*top right*): Betyl depicted between two palms (Dalman 1908: 177); C (*center left*): Altar between two palms (Dalman 1908: 245); D (*center right*): Palm leaf decorating a Nabataean capital of the Ḥegra facades (Photo Z. Al-Salameen); E (*bottom*): Floral decorations on pottery (Hammond 1959: 375–77)

257

Al-Salameen Plate 2: A (*top*): Part of the Nabataean mural painting of the 'Painted House', Bayḍa; B (*bottom left*): Female head with rosette from Kh. Et-Tannur (McKenzie 2003: Fig. 189); C (*bottom upper right*): Rosettes from Ḥegra; D (*bottom lower right*): Pseudo-Doric frieze with busts and rosettes from Kh. Et-Tannur (McKenzie 2003: Fig. 187)

Al-Salameen Plate 3: A (*top left*): Eagle depicted on a Nabataean facade in Ḥegra; B (*top right*): Stele with an eagle above it, Petra (Patrich 1990: 108); C (*center left*): Eagle depicted on a Nabataean facade in Ḥegra; D (*center right*): Sculpture of eagle wrestling with a serpent (McKenzie 2003: Fig. 186); E (*bottom left*): Panel with the bust of Atargatis (Zayadine 2003: Fig. 41); F (*bottom right*): Nabataean eye-idol (Lindner 1988: fig. 5)

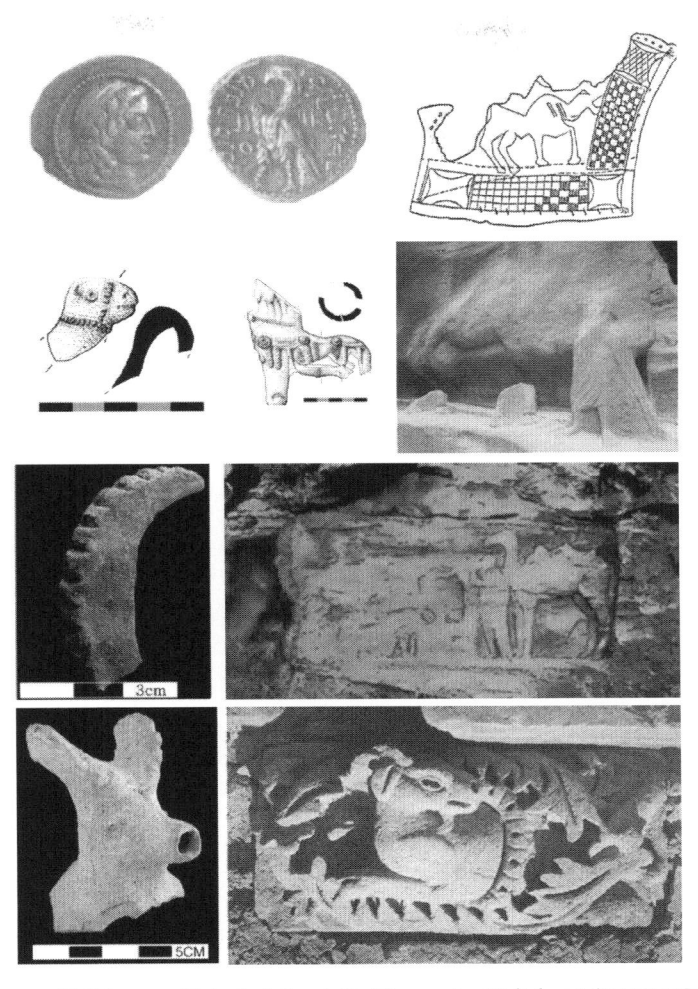

Al-Salameen Plate 4: A (*top left*): Silver coin, Malichus I (35/34 BCE) depicting an eagle (Meshorer 1975: n.12); B (*top right*): Coffin-cloth from Kh. edh-Dhariḥ (Kh. edh-Dhari Exhibition Catalogue 2002: 75); C (*left*) and D (*center*): Fragments of terracotta figurines representing a camel (Tuttle 2009: 452, 471); E (*right*): Camel relief in the Siq in Petra; F (*left*): Fragment of a terracotta figurine representing an ibex head (Tuttle 2009: 515); G (*right*): Camel relief near the Monastery, Petra (Dalman 1908: 276); H (*bottom left*): Fragment of a terracotta figurine representing an ibex head (Tuttle 2009: 520); I (*bottom right*): Sculptured ibex head (Glueck 1937: fig 12)

Al-Salameen Plate 5: A (top *left*): Zeus-Haddad with bulls (Zayadine 2003); B (*top center*) and C (*top upper right*): Niches from Petra (Dalman 1908: 310, 312); D (*top lower right*): Lintel from Oboda (Patrich 1990: 94); E (*center left*) and F (*center right*): Lion reliefs from Petra; G (*bottom left*) and H (*bottom right*): Lion-spouted fragments (Glueck 1937: fig. 12)

Al-Salameen Plate 6: A (*top left*): Two lions between a rosette on a façade of Ḥegra; B (*top right*): Winged lion surmounting a Nabataean pediment in Ḥegra; C (*center left*): Depiction of a snake and a horse from Petra; D (*center right*): Winged creature from Petra; E (*bottom*): Rock-cut façade at Ḥegra (photos Z. Al-Salameen)

262

Al-Salameen Plate 7: A (*top*): Personification of the 'fish goddess' (McKenzie 2003: Fig. 192); B (*center*): Elephant-headed capital, Petra; C (*bottom left*): The tholos of the Treasury, Petra; D (*bottom upper right*): The Snake Monument, Petra; E (*bottom lower right*): Panther sculpture (Glueck 1937: fig. 11)

263

Al-Salameen Plate 8: A (*top left*): Terracotta figurine of a woman with raised hand (Tuttle 2009: 374); B (*top right*): Sculptured relief on the Treasury representing a horse and rider; C (*bottom left*): Reverse of a bronze coin with a palm of the hand, Malichus I (34/33 BCE) (Meshorer 1975: n.17A); D (*bottom right*): Reverse of a bronze coin with a standing woman, Obodas III (13/12 BCE) (Meshorer 1975: n.35)

Harrak Plate 1: BL. OR. 8729 (Hatch 1946: Plate XCII)

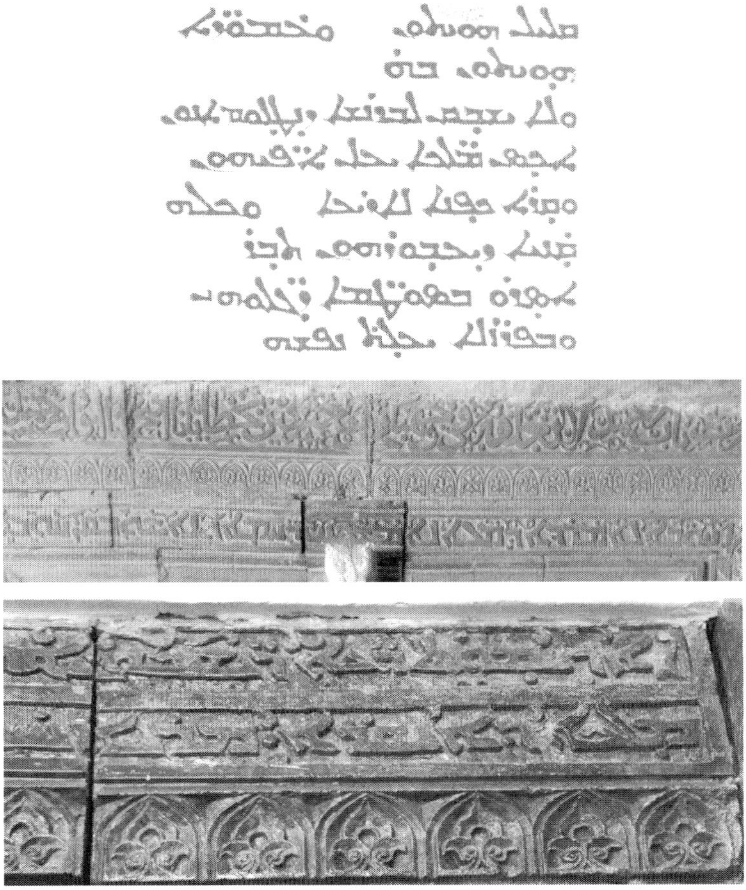

ܡܠܠ ܗܠܝܢ ܥܡܗܘܢ܂ ܘܚܙܒܪܐ
ܗܘܘ ܒܗ ܥܡܗܘܢ܂
ܘܠܐ ܪܓܫ ܠܚܕ ܡܢܗܘܢ܃ ܐܠܐ ܠܗܘ
ܒܠܚܘܕ ܕܩܬܠ ܚܠ ܦܪܨܘܦܗ܂
ܘܡܢ ܗܦܟ ܠܥܠܝܐ ܘܗܘܐ
ܒܝܬ ܘܒܓܒܪܘܗܝ ܠܐܕܐ
ܘܟܠ ܕܗܘܐ ܠܥܠܝܐ ܫܡܥܘ
ܘܚܕܝܘ ܠܕܠܗܐ ܒܗܕܐ

Harrak Plate 2: A (*top*): Add. 17256 (partial Serṭo text) (Wright 1870: CCIX, pp. 142–3); B (*center*): Monastery of Mār-Behnām (South gate); C (*bottom*): Monastery of Mār-Behnām (Exterior wall, Sanctuary)

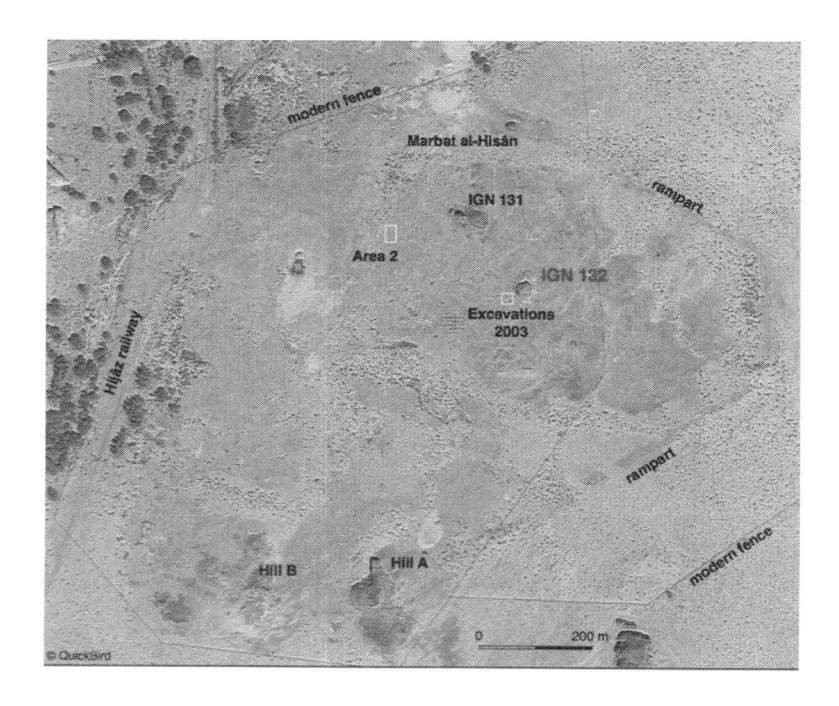

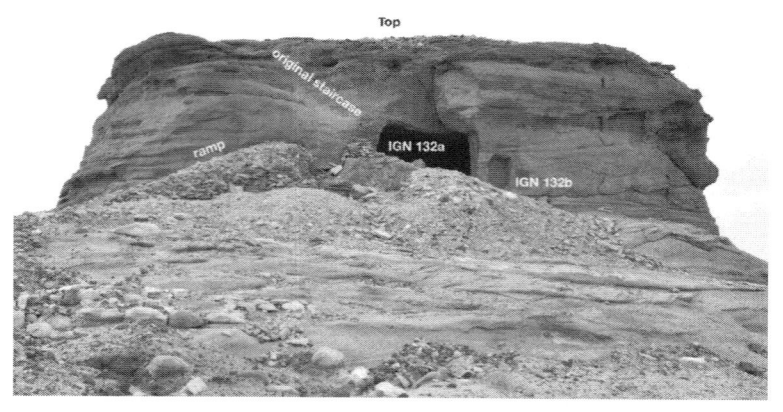

Nehme Plate 1: A (*top*): General aerial view of the residential area of Madâ'in Sâlih with the features mentioned in the text; B (*bottom*): General view of IGN 132 from the west, before excavation

Nehme Plate 2: Kite view of IGN 132 at the end of the 2011 excavation season

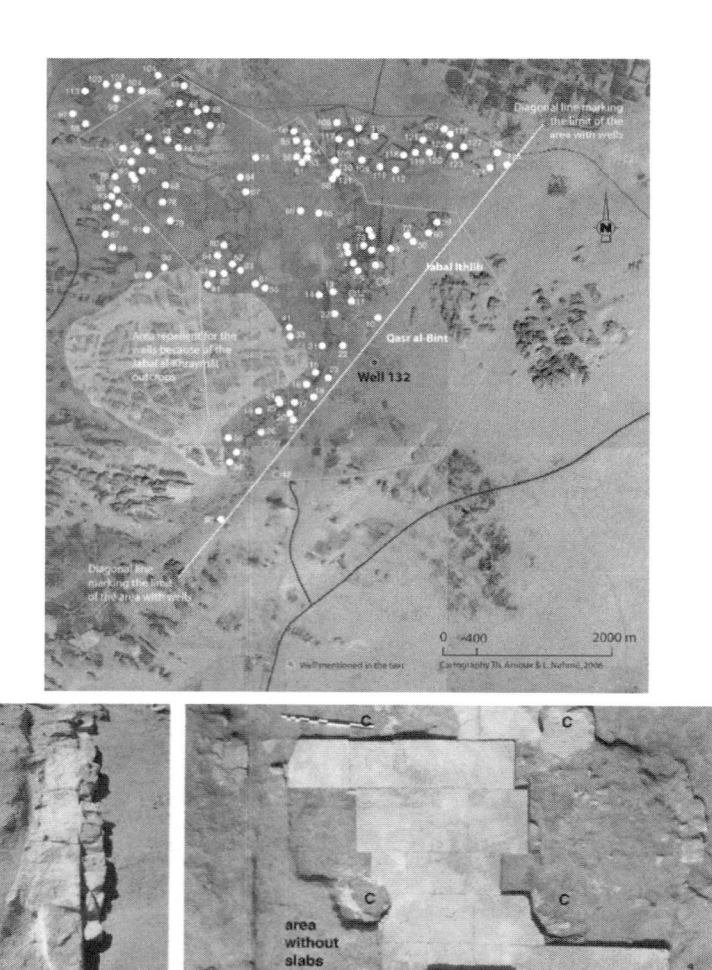

Nehme Plate 3: A (*top*): Distribution of the wells in Madâ'in Sâlih and location of the new well, no. 132; B (*bottom left*): A section of the low wall which surrounds the open-air enclosure on top of IGN 132; C (*bottom right*): Kite-view of the paved platform. The negative of the columns is marked by a 'c'

Nehme Plate 4: A (*top*): The rock-cut chamber IGN 132a and the ramp built with splinters resulting from the digging of the chamber; B (*center left*): General view of Dalman no. 520 from the south; C (*center* right): The southern staircase leading up to the top of Dalman no. 520, from the west; D (*bottom left*): Bronze figurine representing an eagle, 60704_M01; E (*bottom right*): Bronze casket 60681_M01, with detail of one of the feet

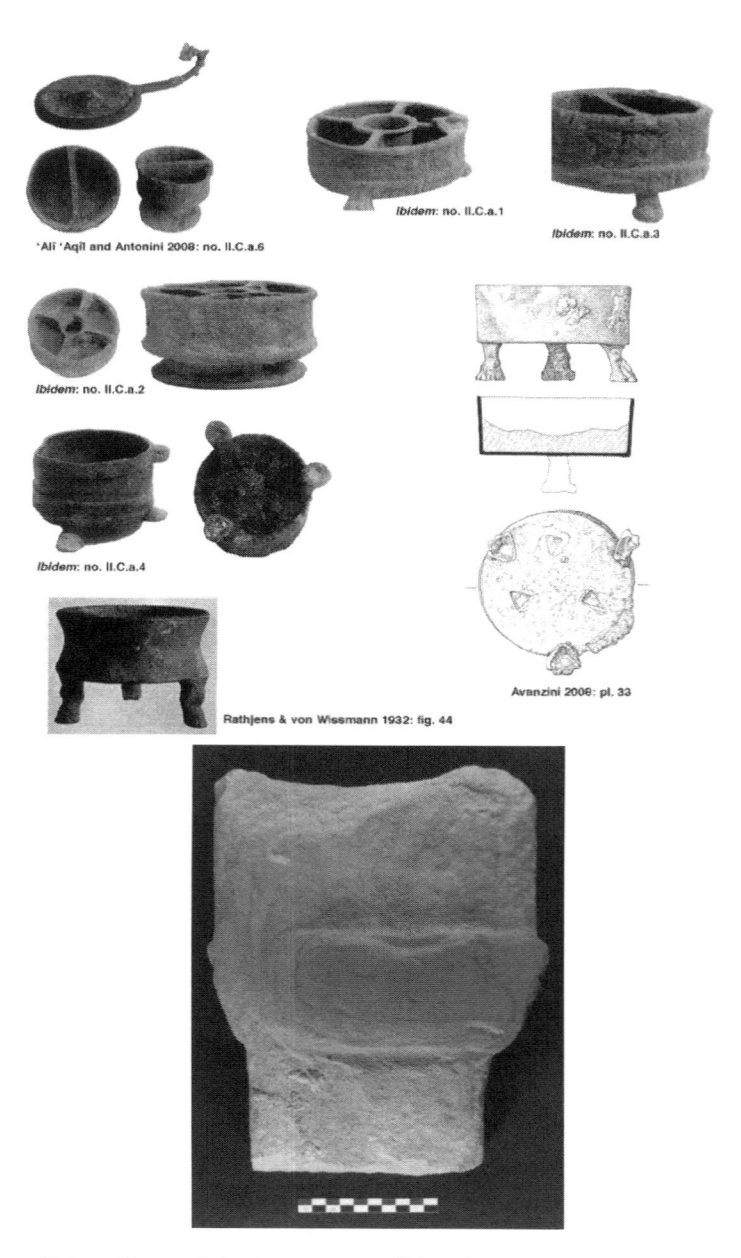

Nehme Plate 5: A (*top*): Yemeni parallels to bronze casket 60681_M01; B (*bottom*): Stone incense-burner 60653_S01, face

RS 18.113A

RS 18.113 [B]

0 3 cm

Pardee Plate 1

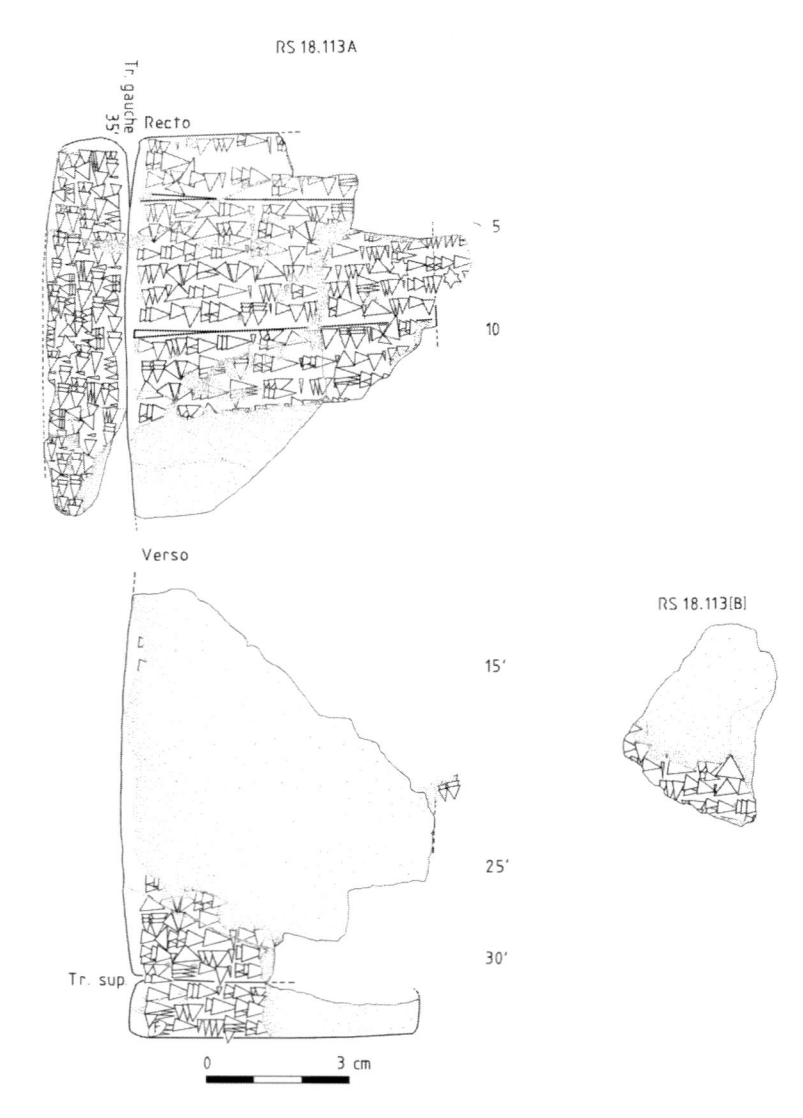

Pardee Plate 2

273

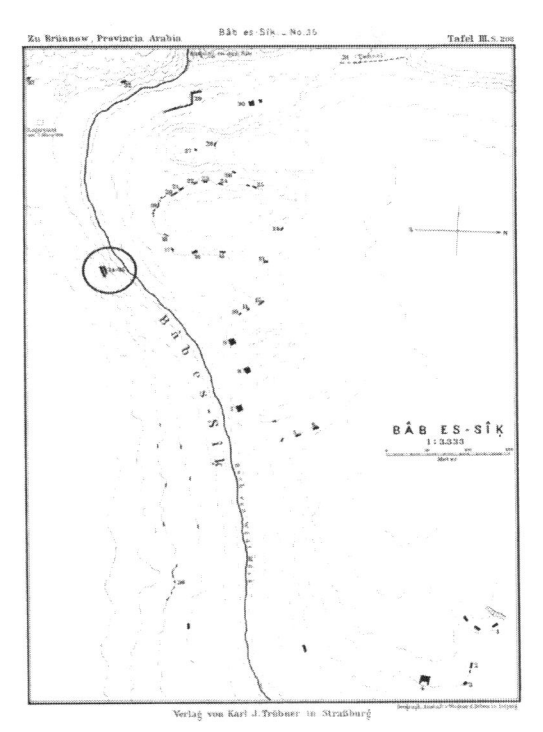

Wadeson Plate 1: A (*top*): Map of the Bāb al-Sīq area showing the location of the Obelisk Tomb and Bāb al-Sīq Triclinium (circled), Petra (Brünnow and von Domaszewski 1904: Pl. 3); B (*bottom*): The Obelisk Tomb and Bāb al-Sīq Triclinium, as seen upon entering the Bāb al-Sīq, Petra (photo A. Hamm)

Wadeson Plate 2: A (*top left*): The façade of the Obelisk Tomb, Petra; A (*top right*): A nefesh carving on the façade of Tomb Br. 320, Wādī al-Thughrah, Petra; C (*bottom*): The statue in the façade of the Obelisk Tomb, Petra (photos L. Wadeson)

Wadeson Plate 3: A (*top left*): Rock-cut features in front of the Obelisk Tomb, Petra (facing west); B (*top right*): Plan of the Obelisk Tomb, Petra (McKenzie 1990: Pl. 124); C (*bottom left*): The burial chamber of the Obelisk Tomb, with a loculus to the left of the arcosolium; D (*bottom right*): The arcosolium in the burial chamber of the Obelisk Tomb, Petra (photos L. Wadeson)

276

Wadeson Plate 4: A (*top left*): The dressing of the walls and ceiling of the Obelisk Tomb (view towards top left corner of chamber); B (*top right*): Plan of the Bāb al-Sīq Triclinium, Petra (McKenzie 1990: Pl. 128); C (*bottom*): The Obelisk Tomb and Bāb al-Sīq Triclinium, Petra (photos L. Wadeson)

277

Wadeson Plate 5: A (*top left*): The interior of the Bāb al-Sīq Triclinium (view towards back wall), Petra; B (*top right*): The small chamber to the right of the Bāb al-Sīq Triclinium; C (*bottom left*): The nefesh carving in the left wall of the chamber to the right of the Bāb al-Sīq Triclinium (note circular receptacle carved in the floor below); D (*bottom right*): The Bāb al-Sīq inscription and its relation to the Obelisk Tomb, Bāb al-Sīq, Petra (photos L. Wadeson)

Wadeson Plate 6: A (*top left*): Detail of the Bāb al-Sīq inscription; B (*top right*): The Bāb al-Sīq inscription and the cavity below it; C (*bottom left*): Double Pylon Tomb Br. 779 after excavation, al-Khubthah, Petra; D (*bottom right*): The burial chamber of Tomb Br. 779 after excavation, with an arcosolium in the back wall and floor graves in the south-eastern corner (photos L. Wadeson)

Wenning Plate 1: A (*top left*): Northeastern corner; B (top right): Northwestern corner; C (*bottom left*): The peak with the Snake Monument, looking southeast; D (*bottom right*): Snake Monument and the rest of the original peak to the right, looking to the northwest (photos R. Wenning)

280

Wenning Plate 2: A (*top left*): D. 47d; B (*top right*): The back wall of chamber D. 210; C (*bottom left*): The snake on the pedestal in chamber D. 210 and two niches above; D (*bottom right*): The draped female figure at the pedestal (photos R. Wenning)

Wenning Plate 3: A (*top left*): 8 Fig. 9 Petroglyph from Umm al-Biyāra (photo U. Hübner); B (*top right*): Wādī al-Qanṭara, rock with the snake relief (photo R. Wenning); C (*bottom left*): Fig. 11 Votive niche in the Wādī al-Qanṭara (photo D. Kühn); D (*bottom right*): Votive niche on the steps towards Umm al-Biyāra (photo S. G. Schmid)

282

Wenning Plate 4: A (*top left*): Two niches above the snake relief; B (*top right*): Jabal al-Barra, snake relief with inscriptions to both sides and a niche; C (*center left*): Left inscription; D (*bottom left*): Right inscription; E (*bottom right*): Secondary niche in the snake relief (photos R. Wenning)